Jim
BROWN

JIM BROWN
Football Great & Actor

by Marty Gitlin

Published by ABDO Publishing Company, PO Box 398166, Minneapolis, MN 55439. Copyright © 2014 by Abdo Consulting Group, Inc. International copyrights reserved in all countries. No part of this book may be reproduced in any form without written permission from the publisher. SportsZone™ is a trademark and logo of ABDO Publishing Company.

Printed in the United States of America,
North Mankato, Minnesota
102013
012014

Editor: Holly Saari
Series Designer: Christa Schneider

Library of Congress Control Number: 2013946584

Cataloging-in-Publication Data

Gitlin, Marty.
 Jim Brown: football great & actor / Marty Gitlin.
  p. cm. -- (Legendary athletes)
Includes bibliographical references and index.
ISBN 978-1-62403-128-1
1. Brown, Jim, 1936- --Juvenile literature.   2. Football players--United States--Biography--Juvenile literature.   3. African American football players--United States--Biography--Juvenile literature.   4. Running backs (Football)--United States--Biography--Juvenile literature.   1. Title.
796.332/092--dc23
[B]

                                        2013946584

TABLE OF CONTENTS

By the 1964 NFL Championship Game, Jim Brown had proven to be one of the best running backs in the league's history.

Rushing to a Championship

It was December 27, 1964. Christmas had come and gone. But the Cleveland Browns had not earned the gift they yearned to present to their city. They wanted to give it a National Football League (NFL) championship to cherish forever.

Nearly 80,000 chilled fans packed Cleveland Municipal Stadium to watch the Browns battle the Baltimore Colts in the title showdown. Most believed the Colts would easily win. They had steamrolled to a 12–2 record in the regular season. Plus, they had Johnny Unitas, one of the greatest quarterbacks to play the game.

But Cleveland boasted one of the most dominant running backs to ever grace a football field. That man was Jim Brown. Brown's amazing combination of speed and power would forever alter the history of the sport. And he was just about to take over the game.

The Browns led 3–0 in the third quarter. Their defense had shut down the highly praised

Taking a Beating

According to one Brown biography, Baltimore players abused Brown badly during the 1964 championship showdown: "Colts players would step on his hands and kick him in the legs or ribs. Hands and fingers probed through his face mask, which had two bars that protected the lower portion of his face, leaving the eyes exposed, and the Colts attempted to gouge them out. All of the abuse and pain only served to make Brown angry."[1]

Colts attack. Now it was time for their offense to score a touchdown. Everyone wearing a blue Baltimore uniform knew Brown was going to get the ball. Opponents had been targeting Brown since he arrived in Cleveland in 1957. But they just could not stop him.

Brown took a three-point stance and placed his left hand on the muddy turf. At the snap of the ball he bolted left and snagged a pitch from quarterback Frank Ryan. His powerful legs began churning. He followed the blocks of offensive linemen Monte Clark and Gene Hickerson, who had rolled in the same direction to escort him down the field. The Browns were running their famed sweep play. Brown burst through the holes opened by his linemen. Then he picked up speed and raced downfield.

He was finally tackled on the Baltimore 18 yard line after a 46-yard gain.

That play changed the game. The Browns took the momentum and ran with it. They scored a touchdown to stretch their lead to 10–0, soon followed by another to make it 17–0.

Brown was not done playing the role of hero. Late in the third quarter, he caught another pitch from Ryan. This time the sweep was heading right. But the Colts had it covered. They swarmed Brown, but it did not matter. He blasted through one tackler who tried to cut him down at the knees. He kept his feet inbounds as he ran along the right sideline and shed another Baltimore defender attempting to wrap up his shoulders. His 23-yard jaunt set up a field goal that put Cleveland ahead 20–0.

Joyous Jim

At the end of the game, fans rushed the field to tear down the goalposts in celebration of the Browns' 27–0 victory. That win remains one of the most stunning upsets in NFL history. It would not have been possible without the efforts of the great Jim Brown, who had rushed for 114 yards.

In the joyous Cleveland locker room after the win, the media saw a different side of Brown than they had been used to. Brown was usually a bit cold to reporters and guarded with his answers. But not on this happy occasion. "It's the biggest thrill of my career," he said. "I have had better days as an individual, but this is the most satisfying of all."[2]

Brown also yearned to share that satisfaction with those who helped contribute to the victory off the field. He sent a telegram to Forman Collier, wife of Browns coach Blanton Collier. Brown thanked the woman for allowing her husband to spend the time necessary to groom the team into champions.

The Browns and their fans might not have been rejoicing had Brown not run wild during the 1964 regular season. Brown averaged just 4.2 yards per rushing attempt as the Browns won three of their first five games. He then exploded to average 6.4 yards per carry and ran for 661 total yards as they

The Uncalled Touchdown

The Browns scored three touchdowns in their stunning 27–0 defeat of Baltimore in the 1964 NFL Championship Game. All were passes from quarterback Frank Ryan to Gary Collins. It appeared Brown scored a fourth touchdown in the fourth quarter. Brown leapt toward the end zone, but the referees ruled that the ball never crossed the goal line. The Browns had to settle for a field goal.

Soon after the 1964 NFL championship, Brown was named the S. Rae Hickok Professional Athlete of the Year for 1964.

won their next five contests. His performance was pivotal in the team's run to the Eastern Conference championship. In the season's final game against the New York Giants, Brown rushed the ball for 99 yards on

20 carries, leading to a 52–20 victory for the Browns. When he heated up, so did the Browns.

Silencing the Critics

Brown had been criticized for not contributing enough as a receiver. But he made up for it with his rushing. Former Browns quarterback and Hall of Famer Otto Graham had complained that year about Brown's blocking and claimed the team would never reach the title game with Brown as the center of the offense. Yet Brown's blocking proved to be a key component in the championship game. "He has scored more touchdowns

Birth of a Movie Career

Brown was voted into the Pro Bowl every season of his nine-year career. His 1964 visit to Los Angeles to participate in the annual NFL all-star game proved more eventful than the others. It launched his movie career.

Brown was asked if he wanted to play a cavalry sergeant in an upcoming Western titled *Rio Conchos*. He replied that he was no actor. Movie studio 20th Century Fox worked to convince Brown to take the part. He agreed to read the script. Brown grew more intrigued by the idea of becoming the first black action hero in a mainstream American film. He eventually accepted the role.

The grand opening of the movie was an event in Cleveland. It was billed as Salute to Jim Brown Night in October 1964. Patrons watched the muscular Brown on the screen as he chased down thieves who had stolen weapons. He was not a polished actor, but neither were most action stars of his time.

and gained more yardage on other occasions, but he never was a greater team player," Ryan said after the win over the Giants. "His blocking was tremendous."[3]

So was Brown's confidence. The Browns were among the few teams that stayed in a hotel the night before home games. The tradition helped the team bond before games. Brown voiced his prediction that the Browns would beat the Colts when he and guard John Wooten were driving together to the hotel the night before the big game.

He was right. But to Brown, the upset over Baltimore did more than give Cleveland a title. He was already one of the biggest stars in American sports, but this was the first time he had led the Browns to a league championship. This new level of fame would allow him to further causes off the field.

No Player of the Year—Just a Champion

It was ironic that Brown was named NFL Player of the Year in 1963 and 1965 but not 1964, the year his team won the championship. The honor that year went to Baltimore Colts quarterback Johnny Unitas, who received 32 votes to Brown's eight. The award was given before the championship game. Brown got a measure of revenge when he led his team to the lopsided win over the Colts for the NFL crown. The Cleveland defense, meanwhile, shut out and frustrated the legendary Unitas.

It would help him take a prominent role in the fight against racism and discrimination. His celebrity status would also allow him to become a leader in the budding black power and black pride movements that were taking hold across the country. He considered those struggles far more important than football.

Brown rushes past defenders in a 1965 game against the
Philadelphia Eagles.

CHAPTER 2

Jim Brown spent part of his childhood in the segregated South.

Strong from the Start

James Nathaniel Brown was born on St. Simons Island off the coast of Georgia on February 17, 1936. James, or Jim as he was usually called, had to navigate his early years without a strong male influence. His father, Swinton Brown, was a professional boxer with a weakness for gambling. Most of his luck was bad. He eventually left his wife, Theresa Brown, Jim's mother, when Jim was only about two weeks old. It would be many years before Jim saw his dad again.

When Jim was two years old, his mother joined the massive black migration from the South to the North—but she did not take her son with her. She gained employment as a housekeeper in Long Island, New York, and promised to send for him one day. She left him to share a small house with his aunt and alcoholic grandmother. He was raised instead by his great-grandmother, who believed in strong discipline. She would beat Jim with a cord if he misbehaved.

Jim began attending school at age four, but not with the white friends with whom he played near his home. In the segregated South, blacks were not allowed to use the same public facilities as whites. So white children attended their own schools, which were superior to black schools. Jim and other black students attended school in a two-room shack. Despite the separation during school hours, Jim remained oblivious to race issues during his early childhood. But he grew increasingly angry as he gained awareness of segregated parks, beaches, and other public spaces.

From Georgia to New York

Both the racism Jim encountered and the rejection he felt from his parents deeply affected him throughout his life. He carried that sense of abandonment even after his mother beckoned him to Long Island, which was not segregated, in 1944. He was eight years old. He had not seen her in six years.

Jim joined his mother in an affluent section of Long Island called Great Neck, leaving behind his home in Georgia. The two of them lived in the home of her employers, who provided them with a tiny room. But they eventually moved to nearby Manhasset, New York, where Jim enrolled in elementary school.

His father, who had also moved to the area, sometimes made surprise visits to their home. But he was not around long enough to stimulate feelings of love and affection from his son. With his mother working shifts as long as 18 hours, Jim was often left alone after school to fend for himself.

An adventurous spirit and temper sometimes got Jim in trouble. He befriended kids who formed a club together. Most of them were fatherless and felt a sense of family within the group they did not have at home. They brawled with others from nearby neighborhoods. Jim earned a reputation as one of their roughest.

He also earned a reputation as a great athlete. Jim and his friends often played tackle football on the hard

Sad Return to St. Simons

Though Jim was only eight years old when he moved from St. Simons Island to New York, he occasionally visited his first home. But one bad experience there in his early twenties had him convinced he would never return. It was while he was attending college and was already a nationally known football star. He traveled to St. Simons to visit his aunt and grandmother, who was working as a housekeeper for a white family.

It was the mid-1950s. Segregation and racism were still rampant in Georgia. Jim's grandmother informed the man of the house she worked at that Jim would be visiting. The man replied that he wanted to meet the football star. So he met Jim at the door, shook his hand, and praised him for his football accomplishments, but he did not invite Jim into his house. Jim assumed he was snubbed because he was black and vowed never to go back to St. Simons. Jim was true to that promise for many years, though he did visit the island later in life.

pavement of side streets littered with broken glass. They sought to prove their toughness as they cut themselves up.

Finding Positive Influences

Despite his participation in sports, Jim was not on a positive life path. He was bored with school. He was following the same path of violence and disrespect for society that had landed many kids in criminal gangs, jail, or worse. If not for a man named Jay Stranahan, the sports world might never have known Jim Brown.

Their relationship began when Jim attended Plandome Road Junior High. He picked up a lacrosse stick out of curiosity and began to play. This caught the eye of Stranahan, a gym teacher at the school who had been teaching lacrosse to Long Island kids for 20 years.

Violent Outburst

Jim had a hard time controlling his anger from a young age. When he was 11, a boy in his neighborhood called him a racist name. Jim said nothing in response. Instead, he punched the boy in the face. Jim would struggle with violence and anger later in his life as well.

Stranahan was intrigued by Jim, who looked quicker and stronger than the other boys. He wanted Jim to play lacrosse for his team.

Other teachers were wary of Jim, whom they viewed as sullen and violent. But Stranahan perceived him as thoughtful and in need of a father figure. He worked to build trust and give Jim confidence by making him aware of his athletic potential. Stranahan eventually won the boy over. Jim emerged as a standout in lacrosse, baseball, and football. He proved wrong those who did not believe in him by soaking in the advice of his coaches and showing them respect.

Jim was no longer directing his anger toward mindless violence. Instead, he was controlling it on the athletic fields and earning the same result—victory over an

Fueled by White Competition?

Ed Corley was one of Jim's friends. The two played sports together when they were young. Corley later said that, early on, Jim did not rise above the other young athletes. "He was exceptional, but a lot of us were exceptional," Corley said. "It wasn't until he started playing around the white players that he became better than everybody. I can't explain why. I think he wanted to prove to whites that he was just as good, if not better, than them."[1]

Sports were a positive outlet for Jim.

opponent. He understood that he could take his energy and aggression and funnel them in a positive direction.

By the time he arrived at Manhasset High School, Jim had grown into a standout athlete. Football coach Ed Walsh sought to help him even more. Walsh had become aware of Jim's athletic ability by watching him around the gym in fifth grade. Walsh was also aware that Jim was a brawler. He agreed with Stranahan that what the boy needed were positive male influences.

Walsh emerged as the most important figure in Jim's life. He helped Jim develop a tremendous work ethic. Walsh embraced his role as a mentor. He showed love and caring that Jim appreciated. Jim became the hardest worker on the team. He even practiced drills alone during lunch period.

Walsh also helped Jim work through issues at home. Even though his parents were divorced, Jim became angry when his mother brought dates over to their house. Jim and his father were not very close, but they had developed a relationship. "My father was restrained from being with us, but the few times I saw him, it was cool," he said. "Basically we made a pact: It was never said, but understood, that he wouldn't do anything for me and I wouldn't do anything for him."[2]

Learning a Valuable Lesson

Young Jim did not appreciate the value of a good education. But he later embraced the notion so strongly that he spoke often about it to kids when he got older. In 2009, he expressed his feelings about his schooling to students in Massachusetts. "I had the best education you could get," he said. "I took advantage of that education and I used it to make myself stronger and make me more than just a big, strong athlete."[3]

His parents would often get into intense arguments while Jim listened in the other room. He would sometimes spend days at a time away from home. Frustrated, he would visit Walsh, who would calm him down. "Ed Walsh . . . showed me what goodness was and I couldn't be fooled by being told it was something else," Brown said to a group of high school students in 2009.[4]

That goodness would help motivate Jim on the gridiron. He would soon take his first major step toward football stardom.

Jim refocused his life with the help of his junior high and high school mentors.

CHAPTER 3

Jim Brown was a standout on the football field.

Dominating the Competition

Ed Walsh did not care about the color of his players' skin. He treated them all the same. Jim felt fortunate during an era of widespread racism and segregation in the United States to have Walsh as his football coach. Jim was also lucky to attend a school in which discrimination was not tolerated. At Manhasset, blacks could date whites during a time when, in 30 of the 50 states, interracial dating was a crime.

The comfort Jim felt in Manhasset disappeared when he traveled elsewhere with his team. The players often heard racial slurs from opposing players. Walsh told them to ignore the taunts. He added that the best revenge was victory. Jim took the advice and led his team to many victories. The combination of speed and power that would destroy defenses in the NFL was evident early in his high school career. He thrived at both running back and linebacker.

Walsh inserted him into the starting lineup as a sophomore, by which time Jim had grown to

Back at School

Jim relived his glory days at Manhasset High School in late April 2013. He returned to speak to students as part of a program called Hometown Hall of Famers. The Pro Football Hall of Fame sponsored the event. Brown told the students that they were fortunate to "live in this kind of community that goes out and hires the best teachers."[1]

6 feet tall and 174 pounds. He averaged 7.4 yards per carry that season and was merely scratching the surface of his potential. He added 20 pounds the next year and averaged an incredible 15 yards per rushing attempt. Jim then averaged 14.9 yards per carry his senior season despite defenses assigning linebackers and safeties to track his every move.

Star in Every Sport

Opposing athletes did not get a break from Jim once the football season ended. He dominated in basketball, lacrosse, and track as well. He shattered the school record by scoring 53 points in one basketball game. Then he broke that mark three days later with 55. No defender could handle his quickness and strength on a lacrosse field. College coaches who considered Jim one of the best lacrosse prospects in the nation began scouting his games.

Jim was attracted to new challenges. He switched from lacrosse to baseball one spring and threw two no-hitters as a pitcher. He was so impressive that the New York Yankees offered him a minor-league contract that he turned down. By the time he graduated, he had earned 13 varsity letters and led the football team to its first unbeaten season in almost three decades.

If not for the urging of Walsh, however, he might not have furthered his athletic career. Jim was highly intelligent but not focused in the classroom. Walsh understood that Jim needed to improve his academic performance to land a college scholarship. Jim listened to his

Best for the Rival

Jim saved some of his best high school football performances for Manhasset archrival Garden City. In one game, he was punched in the stomach while carrying the ball. Jim noted that the player that hit him also played running back on offense. The next time that player got the ball, Jim tackled him so hard he supposedly drove him into a fence several feet from the sideline. In his final game against Garden City, Jim made seven tackles in the last 11 plays of the game to help clinch victory.

mentor. He raised his overall grade to a B average and maintained it.

What Jim had not learned was how to control his temper. He funneled some of his aggression into sports, but teammates and classmates accused him of bullying. He was elected chief justice of a student court, which some believed he used as a green light to punish or intimidate those he felt had broken the rules. Teammate and lifelong friend Ed Corley believed there were two sides to Jim. "Some kids called Jim a bully," Corley said. He continued:

> I personally never saw him go out of his way to do that, but I was also aware that other kids felt he did. I could rely on Jim. He was a great friend who never stabbed me in the back. But he also had a hair-trigger temper. If you riled him or opposed him, he could get very, very angry.[2]

Racism: Perceived and Real

What triggered both anger and fear in Jim was racism. Though he encountered little of it in Manhasset, he perceived racial barriers placed in his way. That perception was one reason he chose to play football in college despite being talented enough to play other sports. Jim believed there were fewer obstacles for black running backs. He received more than 40 offers from college football programs. Ivy League schools also targeted him for his academic and athletic prowess.

Walsh wanted Jim to play for legendary coach Woody Hayes at Ohio State University. He was ready to follow that advice, but a Manhasset lawyer named Kenneth Molloy changed Jim's mind. Molloy was a graduate of Syracuse University, where he had starred in lacrosse. He convinced Jim that he could play both football and lacrosse for the Syracuse Orangemen. Molloy told Jim he could get him a scholarship at the school.

But Molloy did not inform Jim that Syracuse football coaches shied away from signing black players. He knew that Brown would not agree to attend that school if given that information. Molloy believed that once Brown began showing his talent, the coaches would offer him a scholarship. He began a campaign to raise

Taking the Moral High Road

Some college athletic recruiters cheated in their efforts to sway Jim to their school. They illegally offered him money to accept their scholarships. Jim refused. He compared taking money to the plight of blacks in the United States before they were freed from slavery. "I ain't no slave to be bought," he said.[3]

Syracuse football coach Ben Schwartzwalder, *left*, set rules Jim needed to follow in order to be allowed on the football team.

money for Jim's tuition and expenses. He received contributions from the community.

There was one problem. When Syracuse lacrosse coach Roy Simmons confronted football coach Ben Schwartzwalder about Jim, he was told, "Not interested. He's colored."[4] Schwartzwalder later told Walsh he was not prejudiced, but he did not want blacks on his team because "they are too much trouble."[5]

Those words angered Walsh. So did the plan Schwartzwalder outlined to allow Jim to play for Syracuse. Schwartzwalder drew up ten rules. The first on the list mandated that Jim could not date any white

The Sad Story of Avatus Stone

The black player that Ben Schwartzwalder recalled when initially rejecting Jim Brown was quarterback Avatus Stone. Stone was an immensely talented player with the Syracuse Orangemen. But Stone angered the coaches by refusing to abide by their rules against dating white students. He also was not allowed to live or eat with his teammates. Fellow students posted racist notes on his dormitory door. Some even threatened to kill him if he did not quit the team.

After an argument with coaches, during which he claimed he was called racist names, Stone quit the team. He signed to play professionally in the Canadian Football League and performed well for a short time. Schwartzwalder refused to admit that racism drove Stone away from his program. He cited his experiences with Stone in stipulating rules that would allow Jim to play football at Syracuse.

women. Another required that he could not eat or live with his teammates. Jim was not told about his prejudiced coach and insulting rules before attending the college to begin his college football career. A clash between coach and player was inevitable.

Jim went on to play football at Syracuse despite the prejudiced attitude of the football coach.

CHAPTER 4

Jim Brown was the only black freshman on the Syracuse football team.

Life as an Orangeman

Brown was one miserable freshman in 1953. He was buried on the bench of the Syracuse Orangemen football team as the fifth-string running back. He knew that some coaches hated him because he was black. He did not know that he had yet to earn a scholarship. Molloy had paid for his first year at the school with the money he raised.

Brown was irate about not playing but could not verbally express his anger. During one practice, after being ignored once again by the coaches, he lay down on a corner of the field with his arms and legs spread out and remained there for several minutes. On other occasions, he simply stormed off the field into the locker room. He believed that coach Ben Schwartzwalder, who initially balked at the idea of allowing Brown to play for his team, was disrespecting him.

"The first thing my football coach attacked was my talent," Brown said. "He said I couldn't run the ball and that I wasn't any good. I would fight it

Always an Orangeman

Brown has remained involved in Syracuse University through a group called Coming Back Together (CBT). It celebrates the many black and Latino athletes that played at the school. Brown has enjoyed returning to Syracuse as part of CBT and seeing fellow black graduates that had used the school to grow personally and professionally. It has given him a sense of pride in his alma mater.

every day, but finally I thought, 'Maybe he's right; maybe I can't run.'"[1] He was thinking of quitting the team. Manhasset Superintendent of Schools Raymond Collins came to the rescue. He visited Brown and tried to convince him to stay. He assured Brown that his athletic experience would improve and he would get playing time, but then coaches told Collins the only way Brown would play was as a defensive lineman or punter.

Brown might have eventually left the school if not for Syracuse lacrosse coach Roy Simmons. Simmons befriended Brown. When Brown was at his lowest, Simmons raised his spirits. Simmons did not care about the skin color of his players—only that they could compete in lacrosse. Brown remained thankful to Simmons for the rest of his life. "Roy

Simmons is the greatest man I have ever known," Brown said years later. He continued:

> Roy treated me so well during my first season in football that I went out for lacrosse purely because of my affection for him. He's the kind of guy you never want to let down. He was the reason I stayed in school.[2]

Taking Advantage of Opportunities

Still, Brown wanted the chance to display his talent on the football field in his sophomore year. Schwartzwalder refused to give him an opportunity until a rash of injuries to other running backs forced him into the lineup. Brown exploded for a 20-yard run against the University of Illinois but was benched again after fumbling. Syracuse fans wanted to see more of the talented player. However, Schwartzwalder seized every opportunity to yank him off the field.

It took yet another injury for Schwartzwalder to play Brown in a game against the Cornell University Big Red. Brown blasted up the middle for a 54-yard touchdown and finished the game with 151 yards. He exceeded 100 yards and scored twice the following week, dominating the Colgate University Raiders. But after a mediocre performance against the University of Pittsburgh in the 1955 season opener, he was demoted to the second team.

Brown was furious. It took further pleading from Manhasset coaches and friends to convince him to stay at Syracuse. He put his anger to good use. He scored four touchdowns in five carries during a practice that week and injured several defensive teammates with his fierce play. Schwartzwalder placed him back into the starting lineup and kept him there for the rest of his college career.

Doing Everything Well

Meanwhile, Brown was making an impact in every sport in which he participated. He averaged 13.1 points per game for the basketball team during his sophomore and junior seasons. But racism reared its ugly head again. He did not return for his senior year because coaches already had two black starters and

Turning the Page

The experience of having Brown as a student-athlete helped the Syracuse football program move away from discrimination. Brown was soon asked to assist in recruiting more black players. Among those he helped bring to the school were future greats such as running back Ernie Davis and tight end John Mackey. The Orangemen even won a national title in 1959 with contributions from Davis and other black players.

Brown, with fellow Syracuse students, was bandaged after a 1956 game.

refused to add a third. Among them was Vincent Cohen, who claimed the Syracuse basketball team would have won the national title if Brown had played in 1957. Brown relished every opportunity to display his athletic talents. In the 1954 National Amateur Athletic Union Meet, he finished fifth in the decathlon, a competition in which each athlete has to compete in 10 different events.

Lacrosse, however, was perhaps his best sport. Coach Simmons's accepting attitude helped Brown overcome the discrimination around him. Brown simply played better when he received racial taunts from opponents on the lacrosse field. "He was called racial slurs by opponents," said teammate Roy Simmons, son of the coach. "It was constant, every game. The more someone called him a disgusting racial name, the more he scored. He punished teams that used that stuff by embarrassing them on the field."[3]

Brown showed off his skills on the national stage, scoring five goals in the North-South All-Star Game. He tallied 30 goals his junior year and added 43 goals and 21 assists as a senior. He achieved these feats while also

Amazing Afternoon

It was May 1957. Brown was preparing to play in the last lacrosse game of his college career. Syracuse track coach Bob Grieve approached lacrosse coach Roy Simmons and asked if he could borrow the star player for the high jump in a meet against Colgate.

Brown won that event and raced back. He began to change into his lacrosse uniform when he was told he was needed for two more track events. He ran back

to the track, won the discus, and placed second in the javelin throw. Then he sprinted back to the lacrosse field.

If Brown was tired by then, he did not show it. He tallied a goal and three assists to lead Syracuse to an 8–6 victory and clinch its first undefeated season since 1922. His feat amazed teammate Jim Ridlon. "When you're talking about Jim Brown, you're talking about a really great athlete," Ridlon said.[4]

participating in football and track, as well as the Army Reserve Officers' Training Corps. It was no wonder he was selected to the All-American lacrosse team.

Brown also blossomed into a fine student. He finished his college career with a B-plus average and qualified for the dean's list. But it was Brown's athletic talent that had Syracuse three-sport teammate Jim Ridlon in amazement. "Jim Brown made our [football] team," Ridlon said. He went on:

> We wouldn't have been a good team without him. I mean, the other teams really focused on him. I don't remember better athletes than him. I played basketball with him and I played lacrosse with him, and Jim was always the best person on the field in both of those sports.[5]

Though Brown excelled in every sport he played, he understood that his future was in football, partly since there was no professional lacrosse league. He rushed for 986 yards and scored 14 touchdowns as a senior. He peaked in a 61–7 thrashing of Colgate in which he rushed for 197 yards, scored six touchdowns, and booted seven extra points. He had so dominated that at halftime the press box announcer bellowed to the fans, "The score is now Brown 27, Colgate 7."[6]

However, Brown received little national attention. He finished fifth in the Heisman Trophy balloting thanks mostly to eastern voters who had seen him play.

No Trouble in Texas

Syracuse coaches had learned a lot about Brown by the end of his senior season. They knew he would not tolerate being separated from teammates when they visited segregated Dallas for the 1957 Cotton Bowl.

Black players in that city had previously been forced to stay with nearby black families while the white players checked into a hotel. But the Orangemen found a hotel outside of town that accepted Brown.

Some believed eastern football was second-rate. But they learned that Brown was first-rate when Syracuse played Texas Christian University in the 1957 Cotton Bowl. He rushed for 132 yards and three touchdowns in a narrow 28–27 defeat.

There was nothing more for him to achieve at the college level. It was time for him to take his talents to the NFL.

Brown at the 1957 Cotton Bowl

CHAPTER 5

Jim Brown impressed fans during his rookie NFL season.

Playing in the NFL

Brown had at least won over one Syracuse Orangemen coach as the 1957 NFL Draft approached. It was not Ben Schwartzwalder, who claimed that Brown would not reach his peak as a player for four years. It was line coach Rocco Pirro, who was glowing in his recommendation. "He has the speed of the sprinter, the fake and the artistry of a will-of-the-wisp halfback, and the power of a 220-pound fullback," Pirro said. "He's also the deadliest tackler I've ever seen in the secondary defense."[1]

The Cleveland Browns did not care about his defense when they snagged Brown with the sixth pick in the draft on November 27. They would place him at fullback, a running back position for a larger athlete. Brown would remain in that position for the next nine seasons.

Race in the NFL

Brown made an impact on and off the field from the start of his professional career. He sought to give more power to the players in their contract discussions with owners. He even hired an agent to negotiate his first deal with the Browns. It was an era of individual rights and freedoms in the United States, and Brown was among the first players to embrace it. It was also an era of increasing black pride as blacks struggled to obtain equal civil rights. Brown rode that wave as well.

He believed there was much work to do. When he arrived in the league in 1957, he perceived a quota of six or eight black players on each NFL roster. He felt there was usually an even number so white and black players would not have to share a room on the road. He was also convinced that team owners and league officials steered clear of strong-willed black players. Brown wrote the following in his autobiography *Out of Bounds*:

> *The owners were acting in concert with society. Each franchise wanted [mostly] white teams, sprinkled with blacks, so the [mostly] white fans wouldn't [be upset]. Not just any black athletes were wanted. They wanted nice guy blacks, humble blacks, just-glad-to-be-there blacks, lower-pay, work-hard, say-the-sky-was-blue, the-sun-was-shining blacks. Blacks who wouldn't rock the [boat].[2]*

Brown was quite the opposite, which sometimes caused friction between him and legendary Browns coach Paul Brown, who had guided the team to six NFL title-game appearances in the past seven years. Black teammate Len Ford approached Jim Brown in the summer of 1957 and warned him about Paul Brown. Ford told Jim Brown to run plays exactly how the coach wanted because making suggestions about improving plays would only make Coach Brown mad. Ford added that Jim Brown should never start a conversation with his coach because Paul Brown "does all the talking here."[3]

Brown on a Browns Legend

Browns Hall of Fame quarterback Otto Graham retired before Jim Brown joined the team. But Brown met Graham in 1957 and was stunned when told, "Brown, you'll never make it in the NFL."[4] Brown believed Graham was racist after he uttered the same sentiment to talented, young black players Bobby Mitchell, Gale Sayers, and Charley Taylor. All three wound up in the Pro Football Hall of Fame.

When Graham became coach of the Washington Redskins, he claimed there was contention between his white and black players. A group of white players told owner Edward Bennett Williams that such contention did not exist and that Graham was merely stirring up trouble. Brown told the media that Graham was the biggest problem with the losing Redskins. Williams soon fired his coach.

When the two met again years later, Brown noticed a distinct difference in Graham. "He was gracious and kind to everyone, and it was real," Brown wrote. "When a man wants to get himself right, I will never hold a grudge."[5]

A Great Golfer

Brown believed that being a competitive person did not mean hating to lose. It meant working hard to master a skill. That philosophy was on display one summer when he took up golf. He played seven days a week. He practiced before and after every round until his hands bled. People were amazed that he soon recorded a score of 77 for 18 holes, close to what golf professionals shoot. But Brown was not surprised. He knew he had put in the work it took to reach that level.

Taking the NFL by Storm

Still, the relationship between Jim Brown and Paul Brown started well. The coach casually told his rookie that he had earned the starting fullback job after he outran the Pittsburgh Steelers secondary for a 40-yard touchdown in a preseason game. It was a moment he cherished for the rest of his life.

The player justified the faith of his coach. He rushed for 109 yards and two touchdowns in a 21–17 win over the Washington Redskins. He exploded for 237 yards rushing and four touchdowns in a 45–31 defeat of the Los Angeles Rams. He led the NFL with 942 yards rushing and nine touchdowns to earn Rookie of the Year and Most Valuable Player (MVP) honors.

Brown studies plays before a 1958 practice.

The Browns were coming off the first losing season in franchise history. Brown helped turn that around. The 1957 Browns finished the regular season with a 9–2–1 record before losing to the Detroit Lions in the NFL Championship Game.

By 1958, Brown was already intimidating opponents. Before games he stretched and jogged in front of their sidelines to show off his muscular body. He shattered the league single-season rushing record by nearly 400 yards, earning 1,527 total yards in 1958. He exceeded 100 yards on the ground in eight of his 12 games. When the season was over, he was again voted NFL MVP. But Brown was just warming up. "He's just the best back in the league . . . fast as the fastest, hard as the hardest," marveled Rams lineman Glenn Holtzman in November of that year.

He continued:

He gets off to the quickest start of any big man I've ever seen. . . . The only way I've found to stop him is to hit him right at the ankles with your shoulder . . . otherwise it's like tackling a locomotive.[6]

One Influential Man

The "locomotive" proved greatly influential to his black teammates. They began to understand his anger over racial issues, such as the team paying

Working for Pepsi

Brown was a firm believer in blacks taking advantage of business opportunities. He worked after his retirement to help inner-city blacks overcome poverty through economic growth in their communities.

But Brown was already working during his playing career to make money off the field. He traveled in the offseason as an executive and spokesperson for the Pepsi-Cola Company. He studied their methods of advertising and even rode along on delivery trucks to learn about how the company bottled and distributed its product.

for an extra room to avoid black players having to share with their white teammates. He would not allow them to accept discrimination. Brown helped bring a sense of pride to his black teammates. They showed that pride during interviews with the media by acting serious and polite. "I always talk about Jim in terms of power, and I mean power of the mind," said teammate Bobby Mitchell. He went on:

> In terms of community and social issues, he was far ahead of his time. Brown's message was, "I'm a man. Don't disrespect me." Black players in the NFL were not saying that then. As black players signed with the Browns, their attitude changed overnight, they became more proud and defiant. That was Jim. We set the tone across the league for black players.[7]

Brown might not have had such influence over his teammates had he not been so dominant on the field. In the 1959 season, he added eight more 100-yard rushing performances. He ran for 178 yards and scored five touchdowns in a close victory over the Baltimore Colts. At the end of the season, he led the league with 1,329 yards and 14 touchdowns.

Brown also earned a reputation as one of the toughest and most dependable runners in the sport. He was a prime target for opposing defenses. He could absorb vicious hits that would knock other players out of the game. After a hit, he would rise slowly off the

Tough Huff

The most intense personal battles for Brown came against New York Giants middle linebacker and future Hall of Famer Sam Huff. Huff was one of the few players who could occasionally shut down Brown. Huff told *Time* magazine that once after tackling Brown, he leaned over him and shouted, "You stink."[8] After breaking a Huff tackle for a 65-yard touchdown on the next play, Brown jogged past the linebacker and yelled, "How do I smell now, Sam?"[9]

turf, return to the huddle, and then trudge back to his position, only to plow once more through the line when given the ball. Brown later explained that he used his snail's pace after being tackled as a psychological ploy. He thought the extra time made opponents lose their concentration.

Brown's impact on his teammates and the NFL would continue to grow throughout his career. His strong will and progressive attitude would soon begin reaching far beyond the sport of football.

Teammates Bobby Mitchell, *left*, and Brown in 1958

Jim Brown runs with the ball after making a catch in a 1960 game against the Dallas Cowboys.

Leading the Game

The relationship between Jim Brown and coach Paul Brown took a terrible turn in the spring of 1960. Brown had established himself as one of the greatest running backs in NFL history, and he wanted to be paid like it. He had been asking the Cleveland Browns in private, and in vain, for more money. So he told the media that he would be willing to leave football to embark on a boxing career if he did not get a higher-paying contract from the Browns.

Local newspapers began running stories that Brown was offered $150,000 for a two-fight deal. He fanned the flames of those rumors. "I haven't signed for next season and unless it is for what I think it ought to be, I'll quit," he told reporters. "I think a player ought to be paid according to the improvement he shows from one season to the next."[1]

Paul Brown was furious that his star player was negotiating through the media. He did not know if Jim Brown was serious about trading his football cleats in for boxing gloves. But he did know that the team needed its dominating fullback and that fans would be upset if he was not offered more money. So Paul Brown signed the running back to a contract exceeding $30,000 a year. Jim Brown was now the highest-paid player in the NFL.

Brown certainly played like it. In the 1960 season, he led the league in rushing yet again. He was even better in 1961, recording a league-best 1,408 yards rushing (the NFL regular season was only 14 games at the time). He hit his peak in a 45–24 thrashing of the defending NFL champion Philadelphia Eagles. Brown tied a league record by rushing for 237 yards that afternoon. But in typical Brown fashion, he played down the accomplishment. He said:

> I've played some better all-around games this year. I missed a few blocks today, and a couple of times I went the wrong way when I got a good block. The blocking was tremendous. I don't think I ran any better than usual. You always go all out and sometimes you gain and sometimes you don't.[2]

Deteriorating Relationship

Jim Brown continued to go all out despite a worsening relationship with his coach. Paul Brown was considered an innovator in years past. But by the early 1960s, his offense had become outdated. Defenses began predicting what plays the Browns were going to run. The Browns' ground game grew conservative. Jim Brown became wary of running up the middle against defenses prepared to stop him. He wanted to run the famed Browns sweep, which provided him strong blocking and the ability to use his speed and power to break outside.

The result was a disappointing 1962 season for a team that had once dominated the NFL. The Browns finished with a 7–6–1 record. The players believed the mark did not reflect the level of talent on the team.

The Story of Ernie Davis

Perhaps the most emotional relationship Brown had with a teammate during his time in Cleveland was with fellow running back Ernie Davis. The two had much in common. Davis had starred at Syracuse University, where Brown had persuaded him to play. They both excelled in multiple sports. In 1961, Davis became the first black player to win the Heisman Trophy. Brown and Davis also were both first-round draft picks in the NFL. Davis was selected by the Washington Redskins as the number one pick of the 1962 NFL Draft. He was then immediately traded to the Browns.

But Davis never played in the NFL. He was diagnosed with leukemia shortly after being drafted. He faced his disease bravely, but he wrote an article for the *Saturday Evening Post* in which he claimed he was not brave. Davis died in 1963. Brown thought Davis was indeed very brave. "The way he carried himself, the way he did not drown in his own tears . . . the way that he functioned as a human being under all of those conditions was tremendous courage," Brown said.[3]

Jim Brown and other team leaders planned to confront Coach Brown with their concerns.

When new team owner Art Modell learned about the plan, he told them it was not necessary. Modell soon fired Paul Brown and promoted assistant coach Blanton Collier. The players loved their new coach. He was not as distant emotionally. He felt close enough to hug his players when they returned from the field to the sideline.

Running Wild for Collier

Jim Brown felt energized playing for Collier. Some critics claimed Brown's success was largely a result of Paul Brown's brilliance. Jim Brown wanted to prove them wrong—and he did just that in 1963 with the greatest year ever recorded by an NFL running back.

He opened the season by running for 162 yards, recording the only 100-yard receiving game of his career, and scoring three touchdowns in a 37–14 victory over the Washington Redskins. He followed that with a 232-yard rushing performance in a 41–24 defeat of the Dallas Cowboys. After two games, he was averaging an amazing 11.3 yards per carry. He added seven more 100-yard rushing games, including a 223-yard effort in a win against the Eagles.

By the end of the 1963 season, Brown had shattered his own NFL record by rushing for 1,863

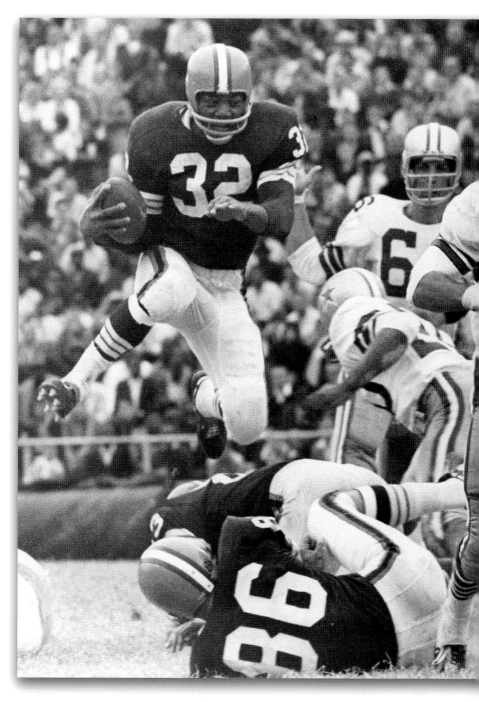

Brown leaps over his teammates while running with the ball in a 1964 game against the Dallas Cowboys.

Great Blocker, Great Man

The teammate Brown gives most credit to for his success is guard Gene Hickerson. Brown was leery when Hickerson was drafted out of the University of Mississippi. Hickerson was from the segregated South, and Brown suspected he might be prejudiced against blacks. But Hickerson did not discriminate against his black teammates. He blossomed as Brown's best blocker. Brown returned the favor years later by helping get Hickerson voted into the Pro Football Hall of Fame. Hickerson was finally elected in August 2007, a year before he died.

yards. Brown gave much of the credit to Collier, who had hired former Browns star receiver Dub Jones to create an offense better suited to the talent. Brown recalled his satisfaction with the changes:

Dub and Blanton were big hits with the guys on offense. They would consult us, listen to us, let us participate in devising plays. Blanton started running me around the ends. He let me catch passes. I even threw some, and if you don't think that was a blast, then you've never played running back.[4]

Open about Race Frustrations

Brown and his team took their momentum and ran with it, winning the NFL championship in 1964. But football was losing its importance to him by that time. He wrote a book that year titled *Off My Chest* in which he not only criticized Paul Brown, but also expressed strong views on race relations in the United States. He recalled a moment in time in which a young white girl wanted to kiss him on the cheek, but he declined because he knew that white adult witnesses would be appalled.

Brown also applauded the growing Black Muslim movement, which had motivated heavyweight boxing champion Cassius Clay to adopt a new religion and change his name to Muhammad Ali. Brown wrote that he understood blacks' anger at white US society. He wrote:

> The first thing the white man must understand, the depth of our protest. Does he realize that the Black Muslim's basic attitude toward whites is shared by almost 99 percent of the Negro population? I protest prejudice, but I am a prejudiced man. The white man has forced me to be prejudiced against him.[5]

The book was the talk of Cleveland. Some praised Brown for his honesty. Others criticized him and even expressed anger. Some fans threatened to cancel their season tickets to Browns games. Brown did not back away from anything he wrote in his book. He told the media that his critics would have no effect on his performance.

Brown had voiced the views of many blacks in the mid-1960s. He was working to empower people

Embracing His Past

Despite the fame and fortune Brown was building as a football star, he remained in tune with the plight of blacks living in poverty. He sometimes drove to the most run-down neighborhoods in the Cleveland ghetto and spent time with the residents. Those trips helped him recall his youth in inner-city New York.

who had been trying to overcome discrimination since blacks first arrived on North American shores as slaves in the seventeenth century. Brown was always more than just a football player. And soon, at the height of his career, he would walk away from the game.

Brown runs with the ball during a game against the New York Giants in 1965.

CHAPTER 7

Brown, *top*, acts in his first movie, *Rio Conchos*. It was released in 1964.

Forging a New Life

Brown was the talk of Cleveland in 1964. He was in the process of leading the Cleveland Browns to the league championship. The merits of his autobiography *Off My Chest* were being debated all over town. He began writing sports columns for the *Cleveland Plain Dealer* newspaper. He was a boxing commentator on the radio and had launched his movie career by starring in *Rio Conchos*.

Yet few anticipated Brown would soon cut his football career short. After all, he was in his prime. He remained the best running back in the NFL in 1965, leading the league with 1,544 rushing yards. He exceeded 100 yards in eight of 14 games and led the NFL in rushing touchdowns with 17. Brown drove his team all the way to the NFL Championship Game, which they lost to the powerful Green Bay Packers. He claimed the bitter cold that day in Wisconsin was the only factor that prevented the Browns from winning their second consecutive title.

Early Retirement

But Brown had been bitten by the acting bug. In June 1966, he was in London filming an action movie called *The Dirty Dozen* when Browns owner Art Modell released a statement to the media. It threatened Brown with suspension if he did not return from England for the start of training camp on July 17. An angry Brown replied in a letter to Modell that he was retiring from football. Brown claimed he had wanted to extend his playing career one more season, but could not work it out with his schedule. Modell later admitted his regret for giving Brown an ultimatum.

Brown indeed quit football and never claimed regret. Other running backs would break his records—records that might have been out of reach had he continued to play. The NFL also expanded its regular season from 14 to 16 games in 1978. He had led the NFL in rushing in eight of his nine seasons and finished his career with a remarkable average of 5.2 yards a carry. But he was ready to move on, citing later that there was more money in acting.

The anger between Brown and Modell did not prevent the Browns owner from honoring him with Jim Brown Farewell Day in January 1967. More than 4,000 fans showed up to a local arena and watched highlights of Brown's career. Among those who flew in to attend were sports icons such as basketball superstar

Bill Russell and heavyweight boxing champion Muhammad Ali. But when it was time for Brown to address the crowd, he did not speak about football. He spoke instead about black people's struggle for economic equality.

Working for Equality

Brown's speech indicated his priorities at the time. Personal wealth was not his only motivation to leave football. He understood that his fame could help raise the status of his fellow blacks across the country. Discrimination and poverty had prevented them from enjoying the fruits of economic development. In the

Brown and the Boxer

In the turbulent 1960s, Brown forged a lifetime friendship with heavyweight boxing champion Muhammad Ali. Brown supported Ali when he refused to join the US Army to fight in the Vietnam War.

Brown was ringside nearly a decade later when an aging Ali battled George Foreman for the heavyweight crown in the African nation of Zaire. Ali knew that Brown, who was filming the fight for his video production company,

had predicted a Foreman victory. Ali looked over at Brown during the fight. He even nodded and winked at Brown while absorbing brutal punches from Foreman.

Ali eventually knocked Foreman out to regain the heavyweight title. And when it was over, he glanced at Brown. "See, Jim?" Ali said. "Told you! Believe me now, Jim?"[1] Ali had gotten what he wanted—Brown's approval.

Racial equality was important to Brown, *left*, and Muhammad Ali, *right*, who contributed to the Negro Industrial and Economic Union.

1960s, frustration over racial inequality boiled over, especially in the inner cities.

Brown helped form the Negro Industrial and Economic Union in 1965 to assist businesses owned by blacks. He believed the best method to achieve overall growth was to empower blacks financially. In 1968, the organization landed a $1 million grant from the Ford Foundation. It also received financial and moral support from such sports legends as Ali and basketball star Kareem Abdul-Jabbar.

The era was one of conflict in the black community. Some followed Martin Luther King Jr.'s message of nonviolence. Others were less patient for change and believed violence was sometimes necessary to evoke change in their communities. Brown took neither side. He explained why

Dabbling in Music

Brown became a jack-of-all-trades in the late 1960s and 1970s. He launched an entertainment management company in Los Angeles that helped the careers of several black musical acts. Included were Friends of Distinction, who exploded onto the scene with pop hit "Grazing in the Grass," and 1970s funk superstars Earth, Wind & Fire.

the Negro Industrial and Economic Union, later called the Black Economic Union, was so important in a 1968 interview:

> We believe that the closest you can get to independence in a capitalist society is financial independence. . . . We've got to get off the emotional stuff and do something that will bring about real change. We've got to have industries and commercial enterprises and build our own sustaining economic base. Then we can face white folks man-to-man.[2]

A New Kind of Black Actor

Brown faced millions of white people on the silver screen. He emerged as one of the most popular action movie actors of the 1960s and 1970s. Author and women's rights activist Gloria Steinem compared him to legendary film star John Wayne.

Brown played a daring character in *The Dirty Dozen*, which proved to be among the most iconic films of its day. He portrayed the sheriff of a small southern town in the movie *tick . . . tick . . . tick*. And he shocked many Americans by playing out love scenes with white actresses such as Raquel Welch in *100 Rifles* and Jacqueline Bisset in *The Grasshopper*. He was breaking down racial barriers.

Brown was thriving in an era in which Hollywood was just beginning to open its doors to black actors.

As an action movie star, he was unlike more sophisticated black actors of the time, such as James Earl Jones and Sidney Poitier. Veteran actor Lee Marvin praised Brown for his work. "He's seemingly more believable to the average Negro than guys like Poitier," Marvin said.[3] Director Robert Aldrich added, "There isn't another Negro actor around quite like Brown."[4]

Taking a New Direction

Brown enjoyed the fruits of his labor. But despite the temptations of fame in Hollywood, he rarely took part in the nightlife. He worked as hard to improve as an actor as he did to maximize his talent on the football field. He stayed in his room and studied his scripts. He sometimes roamed around inner-city Los Angeles to talk to

Scary Incident

Brown met actress and model Eva Bohn-Chin while filming *The Dirty Dozen* in London. It was the beginning of a volatile relationship. In 1968, Brown was arrested after being accused of throwing her off the balcony of their apartment building in Hollywood, California, following a fight. She landed on the concrete below. The incident received much media coverage, but Brown was released after Bohn-Chin refused to press charges. She told investigators that she had fallen off the balcony. Brown maintained his innocence, claiming that she had jumped.

Legal Trouble

More legal trouble arose for Brown in August 1969. He was returning from a golf outing in California when he got into a car accident with 52-year-old Charles Brush. Brush claimed that Brown returned to his vehicle after refusing to present his driver's license. As Brown sped off, Brush claimed he was struck by Brown's vehicle, landed on the hood of the car, and had to hold on to the windshield wipers to avoid falling off. Brush sued Brown for $1.25 million. But a jury did not believe Brush's story. It ruled in favor of Brown, acquitting him of all charges.

black kids about their lives. And he continued to have a lead role in the Black Economic Union.

He was also distancing himself from wife Sue, whom he had married in 1958. The Browns had three children, but he told the media that he was drifting away from his wife because of his movie career. He said:

Sue's a great, great woman. A fantastic woman. But she's not interested in the kind of life I want to live right now. See, she's the kind of woman who likes the kind of man who comes home every evening at a certain hour and shuts the gate on the white picket fence . . . I'm not that kind of man.[5]

The two were divorced in 1972. Brown was changing, but he was also trying to change the world.

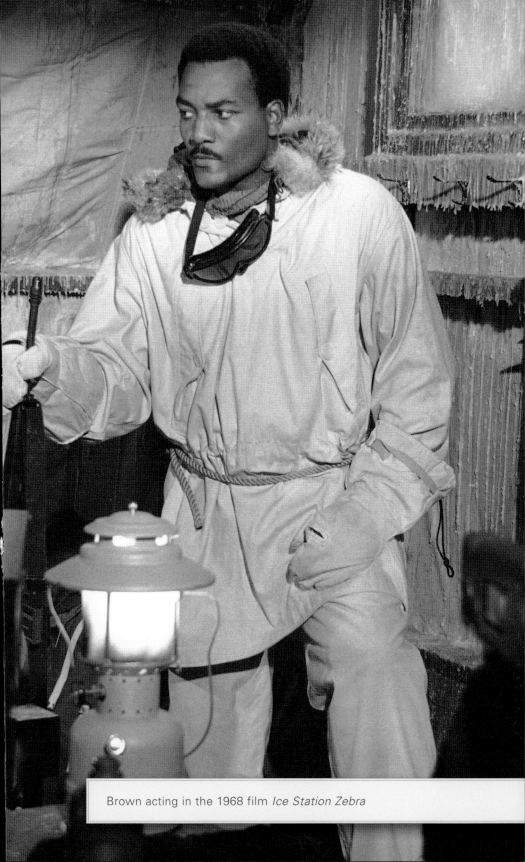

Brown acting in the 1968 film *Ice Station Zebra*

CHAPTER 8

Jim Brown spoke for the need to guarantee all people's rights.

From Movies to Amer-I-Can

Brown made an impact as the first major black action film star and was improving as an actor in the 1970s. He was praised for becoming more believable and versatile on screen, portraying such roles as a Green Beret soldier and a nightclub owner.

Yet Brown never believed he earned the opportunity to blossom. He was landing bit parts instead of starring roles. He felt Hollywood was not ready for a black man like him to take center stage, and he expressed his frustration and anger to the *Cleveland Plain Dealer* newspaper in June 1979. "They don't like me because I can't be controlled," he said. "I've always been outspoken. If too many whites in America love you, you aren't doing anything."[1]

Unsuccessful Business Venture

Brown yearned to give blacks in the entertainment industry a chance he thought they were being denied. So he teamed up with actor

Helping a Friend

Brown had known Richard Pryor for 15 years before the comedian turned to him in 1980 for help with his addiction to cocaine. Brown often drove to Pryor's home, where he tried in vain to convince him to check into a hospital. Pryor eventually attempted suicide by lighting himself on fire and landed in the burn unit of a California hospital. Brown asked him if he wanted to live. Pryor replied that he did. Brown worked to keep Pryor out of the public eye and wean him off drugs. Pryor recovered to return to comedy. He died in 2005.

and comedian Richard Pryor to launch Indigo Productions in June 1983. They intended to give black writers, actors, and producers an opportunity to make small-budget films. Brown was to serve as president of the company, which signed a $40 million contract with Columbia Pictures for funding.

One project Brown sought to produce was *Purple Rain*, a film about the life of rising pop-music star Prince. But Indigo lost that opportunity when Pryor fired Brown and three other Indigo staff members.

Pryor later admitted he had made a mistake by starting the company to begin with. Indigo Productions was defunct within two years.

Launching Amer-I-Can

Brown soon turned his attention to what became his focus and passion for the rest of his life. In 1988, he used some of his own money to launch the Amer-I-Can Program, an extension of the Black Economic Union, to help inner-city black youth. The philosophy of the new organization fit Brown's belief that self-esteem must be raised from within the black community. Before launching the program, Brown consulted with behavior experts, psychologists, educators, ministers, former addicts, gang members, and others to ensure that Amer-I-Can would maximize its ability to assist others. Amer-I-Can elicited the help of teachers to show inner-city youth how to put their time and energy into helping themselves and their neighborhoods.

Brown had already been inviting gang members into his Hollywood home for discussions about how

Almost a Comeback

Brown had been retired from football for 17 years in 1983. He was 47 years old. But Brown was talking about making a comeback. His motivation was Pittsburgh Steelers running back Franco Harris, who was on the verge of breaking Brown's career rushing record of 12,312 yards. Brown, who did not consider Harris worthy of his record, called Oakland Raiders owner Al Davis about a possible job as a running back the following season. He also challenged Harris to a showdown in a 40-yard-dash.

Brown believed he had a good case against Harris. Brown averaged 104 yards rushing per game during his career to Harris's 72.4. Brown also led the league in rushing in eight of his nine seasons. Harris never led the NFL in rushing in his 13 seasons. Brown complained that NFL players had grown soft, claiming Harris would often run out of bounds rather than take a hit from a defensive player. Despite his flirtation with a comeback, Brown did not return to football. Harris never passed Brown's record, but eight players had through the 2012 season.

Brown, *right*, worked for racial equality with friend and civil rights activist Jesse Jackson, *left*.

to end street violence. Those talks intensified as part of Amer-I-Can in 1992 after deadly riots in the inner city of Los Angeles. Through the program, Brown played a role in negotiating a truce between rival gangs that had been killing each other for years. The work of Amer-I-Can even filtered into California jails. There Brown helped inmates control their emotions through lessons in anger management and how to take responsibility for their actions. The prison program helped them become law-abiding citizens upon release.

Soon the program spread to cities throughout the country. It had grown so successful by 1994 that Brown was asked to speak in front of US Senator Herb Kohl and his Subcommittee on Juvenile Justice. Brown told them he was more proud of the achievements of Amer-I-Can than anything he had done on a football field or in front of a camera. In a later interview, he offered that the potential of the program extended beyond the inner cities and prisons. "The beauty of the Amer-I-Can Program is that it is applicable to all people, as it transcends race, age, gender, religion, and socio-economic status," he said. "My belief is that teaching and sharing the program concepts related to self-esteem could significantly impact the problems our society faces today."[2]

Out of Control

Brown helped reduce the violence plaguing youth, but he struggled to tame his

Playing the Small Screen

Brown's movie career stalled in the 1970s, but he did act in several television shows late that decade and into the 1980s. Brown earned parts in such police and detective dramas as *Police Story*, *CHiPs*, and *T. J. Hooker*. He continued to find small acting roles well into the 2000s.

own violent nature. He was charged several times for various criminal offenses, including assault. For years he blamed racism and US society for his anger management problems. He finally admitted his mistakes in his 1989 autobiography *Out of Bounds*, in which he discussed striking former girlfriend Eva Bohn-Chin. He wrote:

> *I have also slapped other women. And I never should have, and I never should have slapped Eva, no matter how crazy we were at the time. I don't think any man should slap a woman. In a perfect world, I don't think any man should slap anyone. . . . I don't start fights, but sometimes I don't walk away from them. It hasn't happened in a long time, but it's happened, and I regret those times. I should have been more in control of myself, stronger, more adult.*[3]

Brown wrote he once felt a sense of power by controlling women. The accomplishments of Amer-I-Can eventually brought him that same sense of power without using violence. Rather than hurting others, he was helping them.

Second Chance at Fatherhood

Earlier in his life, Brown was not a good father to his three kids he had with his first wife, Sue. Son Kevin told filmmaker Spike Lee, who created a 2002 documentary about Brown, that his father had hugged him just once in his life. Daughter Kim also spoke about the lack of attention she received from her dad. "When . . . we really wanted a dad, needed a dad, somebody to talk to . . . it kinda started messing with our heads," she said. "I wanted to be daddy's little girl. I wanted to be held. . . . I wanted him to come to some of my ballet recitals, things like that. And . . . he wasn't there."[4]

Brown got a second chance as a father to two kids with his second wife, Monique, whom he married in 1997. He gave them the affection he failed to give the three children he had with his first wife, Sue. One firsthand witness of Brown's transformation as a father was James Box. Brown had helped Box, who had grown up in poverty, through the Amer-I-Can program. "People

Attention from Lee

One of the most influential black filmmakers in the United States turned his attention to Brown in 2002. Spike Lee created a documentary about Brown's life that year titled *Jim Brown: All American*. The honest portrayal focused not only on his achievements in football, in film, and as founder of Amer-I-Can, but it also delved into Brown's problems with violence against women.

have no idea how good a family man he is," Box said. "When I am in his house, I can't believe sometimes what I'm seeing. He is such a good father, and his household is so different from the one I grew up in."[5]

Brown married his second wife, Monique, in 1997.

CHAPTER 9

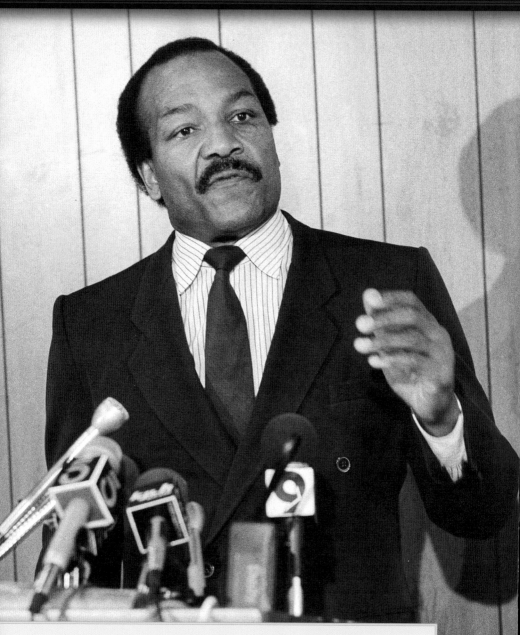

By the late 1980s, Jim Brown had needed to defend himself
several times against criminal offenses.

Back with the Browns

By the late 1980s, negative publicity from Brown's confrontations with police and women began to overshadow his professional achievements. He was becoming a distant memory to many fans who recalled his greatness on the football field. Some in the younger generations knew nothing about him. Brown decided he needed to rebuild his image.

So he called Cleveland Browns owner Art Modell. Nearly two decades earlier, a confrontation between the two had resulted in Brown retiring from the sport he had dominated. They had parted as enemies. Now Brown wanted to be a friend—and Modell embraced him. Brown soon reconnected with the city of Cleveland. He had been critical of Cleveland in the past, claiming it was a racist city. But now, in the hearts and minds of many of its citizens, all was forgiven.

Modell escorted Brown on a tour of the Browns facility. The 1989 Browns were considered to be a Super Bowl contender. Their featured

Backing Republicans

Since World War II, a majority of black voters have cast their ballots for Democrats. But Brown told a writer from *Syracuse University Magazine* in 1996 that he believes the Republicans boast better plans to help the black community. "The Democratic Party encourages dependence [on the government], but the Republican concept makes you get off your [butt]," he said.[3] Brown added that Republican leaders helped launch his Amer-I-Can program in New Jersey, California, and Ohio.

back was Kevin Mack, whose combination of speed and power mirrored Brown's explosive style. Yet when Brown saw Mack in the locker room, he could not help taking a verbal jab at him. Brown registered the same complaint about Mack that he had about many of the modern players. He did not believe Mack was tough enough. "Quit running out of bounds," Brown told Mack as they shook hands.[1] Mack was shocked and upset. Browns general manager Ernie Accorsi made certain Mack understood whom he was dealing with. "Before you get angry," Accorsi said to him, "that's the greatest running back in the history of the NFL."[2]

Powerful Mentor

Bill Belichick also felt the new slew of players were soft. In 1993, the future Super Bowl champion coach of the

Brown continued to work for racial equality and equal opportunity for blacks throughout the years.

New England Patriots was coaching the Browns when he decided his rookies needed to learn about the history of the NFL, the franchise, and life as a professional athlete. So he called in Brown to speak to them. Belichick remarked:

My concern with Jim is that as time goes by, people will forget just how important he was to sports and society. . . . He is without question one of the top two or three human beings I have ever met. He makes me proud to know him and proud to be his friend.[4]

The experience proved so beneficial for the young players that Belichick brought Brown back the following year. This time, he showed the rookies a highlight tape of Brown running the ball with the Browns. The rookies could not believe the greatness they were witnessing. Belichick hired Brown as a

Brown and Sutherland

Actor Donald Sutherland has Brown to thank for keeping his acting career alive. The two met on the set of *The Dirty Dozen* in 1966. Brown later loaned Sutherland $3,000 so he could continue acting. Sutherland went on to make more than 100 films. He never forgot Brown's act of kindness. The two have maintained a close friendship. In 2006, Sutherland attended a surprise seventieth birthday party for Brown.

special consultant, but the position would not last for long. The team was moved to Baltimore in 1996 and became known as the Ravens.

In 1999, the NFL awarded a new team, also called the Browns, to Cleveland. Brown remained passionately tied to the team for years after. New owner Al Lerner hired him as an executive adviser to players and coaches. But Brown felt the sting of disrespect in 2010 after the arrival of new president Mike Holmgren, who had been a legendary coach with the Green Bay Packers. Holmgren reduced Brown's role with the team. The 73-year-old Brown felt so insulted that he boycotted a ceremony in which he was to be inducted into the team's Ring of Honor, a hall of fame for players who have played for Cleveland.

Jail Time

In 1999, Brown was charged with vandalizing the car of his second wife, Monique. Brown refused to accept counseling and community service after the incident and landed in a Los Angeles jail in 2002. Brown claimed the judge picked on him because he was a celebrity. To make a point, Brown embarked on a hunger strike that lasted about three weeks. A prison spokesman claimed his actions were a spiritual cleansing that did not indicate a protest. But Brown told *New York Times* reporter Mike Freeman that though it was indeed a "spiritual fast," his sentence was "wrong, mean-spirited, and not justice."[5]

Back with the Browns

The rift between Brown and Holmgren proved upsetting to Randy Lerner, who had taken over ownership of the Browns after the death of his father. Lerner could not repair the relationship. It was not until Lerner sold the team to Jimmy Haslam in 2012 that Brown found himself in the good graces of the Browns again. Haslam announced in May 2013 that Brown had been hired as a special adviser. His role would be as a link from the team to the community and as a mentor to Browns players.

Outspoken Brown

Brown has never been afraid to speak what he perceives as truth. But his words before the 2012 NFL Draft angered many Cleveland Browns fans. Brown made headlines when he called University of Alabama running back Trent Richardson ordinary. Many experts considered Richardson to be the best running back coming into the league that season.

The Browns traded up to draft Richardson. Brown later backtracked, claiming that he made his statement only to motivate Richardson. And when Richardson scored two touchdowns in a game at Cincinnati, including one in which he broke or evaded four tackles, Brown expressed joy. He also claimed surprise at the attention his criticism of Richardson had received. "It was like a firestorm coming out of the mountains. There is no disrespect in waiting to see a person prove himself," he said. "Now, the great thing sitting here today is that I saw a flash of the talent and I loved it."[6] However, the Browns traded Richardson to the Indianapolis Colts just two weeks into the 2013 season.

At a press conference on May 29, 2013, Jimmy Haslam, *right*, announced Brown would be a special adviser to the Browns.

When Haslam made the announcement, he spoke glowingly of Brown. His words reflected the feelings of older Browns fans, who could still recall Brown carrying would-be tacklers into the end zone. "He's . . . the most famous Cleveland Brown of all time and best player that's ever played here," Haslam told the media. "One of the reasons the Browns remain so popular is when a lot of us were growing up, they followed [him] and he was their hero."[7]

Brown was indeed still a hero to millions. Even those who admired him, however, understood he was a flawed and complex man. His temper and arrogance sometimes got him in trouble. His pride often got the best of him. But he made an impact, not only as perhaps the greatest football player to ever don a pair of cleats, but as an activist who fought to improve the lives of all blacks. Nothing he achieved on the gridiron was more important to him than that.

Brown attended the Cleveland Browns' training camp in August 2013.

TIMELINE

1936

James Nathaniel Brown is born on February 17 on St. Simons Island off the coast of Georgia.

1944

Brown moves from Georgia to New York to rejoin his mother.

1953

Brown begins attending Syracuse University.

1957

Brown earns the NFL Rookie of the Year and MVP honors after rushing for a league-leading 942 yards.

1958

Brown shatters the NFL single-season rushing record with 1,527 yards and earns his second MVP Award.

1958

Brown marries his first wife, Sue.

1954

Brown averages 5.9 yards per carry as a sophomore on the Syracuse University football team.

1956

After rushing for 986 yards and 13 touchdowns as a Syracuse senior, Brown earns All-America status.

1956

On November 27, Brown is taken with the sixth pick in the NFL Draft by the Cleveland Browns.

1960

After demanding more money, Brown receives a $30,000-a-year contract with the Browns, becoming the NFL's highest paid player.

1963

Brown breaks his own single-season rushing record with 1,863 yards and earns his third MVP honor.

1964

Brown rushes for 114 yards to help the Browns defeat the Colts to win his only NFL Championship Game.

1964

1964

1965

Brown launches his acting career in the Western *Rio Conchos.*

Brown's first autobiography, *Off My Chest*, is released.

Brown wins his fourth NFL MVP Award by rushing for 1,544 yards and scoring a career-high 21 touchdowns.

1988

1989

1994

Brown launches the Amer-I-Can program to help poor and troubled youth.

Brown's second autobiography, *Out of Bounds*, is published.

Brown speaks to the US Congress about the success of his Amer-I-Can program.

1965

Brown helps form
the Negro Industrial
and Economic
Union in 1965 to
assist businesses
owned by blacks.

1966

Brown retires from
the NFL in July.

1968

Brown is accused
of throwing Eva
Bohn-Chin off a
balcony in June,
but the charges are
dropped.

1997

Brown marries
his second wife,
Monique.

2007

Brown opts for jail
over community
service for smashing
wife Monique's car
after a fight.

2013

Brown is hired
as special adviser
to the Browns by
new owner Jimmy
Haslam.

ESSENTIAL FACTS

DATE OF BIRTH

February 17, 1936

PLACE OF BIRTH

St. Simons Island, Georgia

PARENTS

Theresa and Swinton Brown

EDUCATION

Manhasset High School (1949–53)

Syracuse University (1953–57)

MARRIAGES

Sue James, 1958 (divorced, 1972)

Latifa Monique Gunthrop, 1997

CHILDREN

With Sue: Kim, Kevin, Jim Jr.

With Monique: Aris, Morgan

CAREER HIGHLIGHTS

Jim Brown was honored as the NFL's Rookie of the Year in 1957 and MVP in 1957, 1958, 1963, and 1965. He led the NFL in rushing in eight of his nine seasons, breaking the single-season records in 1958 and 1963. Brown led the Browns to an NFL championship in 1964 and retired as the league's all-time leading rusher.

SOCIAL CONTRIBUTIONS

Throughout his collegiate and NFL career, Brown broke down barriers for black athletes, working to end discrimination in sports. He was a vocal opponent of racism and discrimination in the NFL. He became the first black action film hero in the 1960s, opening doors for black actors to receive more roles in the genre. In 1988, he launched the Amer-I-Can program, through which he has helped thousands of troubled youths turn their lives around.

CONFLICTS

Brown has struggled to control his violent nature, particularly against women. He has been charged several times for various criminal offenses, including assault. He struck former girlfriend Eva Bohn-Chin and was charged with vandalizing the car of his second wife, Monique.

QUOTE

"It's the biggest thrill of my career. I have had better days as an individual, but this is the most satisfying of all."—*Jim Brown, on winning the 1964 NFL championship*

GLOSSARY

affluent
Wealthy.

assault
A physical attack on an individual or group.

discrimination
Unfair treatment of a person or group based on a particular
trait, such as race or religion.

draft
A system in sports in which each team in a league selects an
incoming player. The order of picks is generally determined
by the regular-season record, with the worst teams
picking first.

gridiron
A football field.

Heisman Trophy
The award given annually to the best college football player.

intimidate
To make someone take an action by threats or fear.

mentor
A trusted counselor or teacher.

pitch
A backward toss from a quarterback to a running back.

prejudice
An unreasonable attitude of hostility directed at another
person due to race, sex, religion, or other characteristic.

racism

Prejudice against another person based on characteristics such as skin color or nationality.

recruit

To try to get players from a lower level, such as high school, to play for a higher level, such as college.

rush

In football, to advance on the field by running with the ball.

scholarship

Money awarded to a student to help pay for school. Great athletes are sometimes given athletic scholarships in order to represent a school through its sports teams.

segregation

The separation of people based on race, religion, or other traits.

sweep

A play in football in which the offensive linemen run wide to the outside to block for the running back.

upset

A victory by a team not favored to win.

ADDITIONAL RESOURCES

SELECTED BIBLIOGRAPHY

Brown, Jim, with Steve Delsohn. *Out of Bounds*. New York: Kensington, 1989. Print.

Freeman, Mike. *Jim Brown: The Fierce Life of an American Hero*. New York: William Morrow, 2006. Print.

Toback, James. *Jim: The Author's Self-Centered Memoir on the Great Jim Brown*. Garden City, NY: Doubleday, 1971. Print.

FURTHER READINGS

Anderson, Jennifer Joline. *The Civil Rights Movement*. Edina, MN: ABDO, 2012. Print.

Gitlin, Marty. *Cleveland Browns*. Edina, MN: ABDO, 2011. Print.

Murray, Jim, and Gabriel Schechter. *Guts and Glory: The Golden Age of American Football*. Los Angeles: Taschen, 2011. Print.

WEB LINKS

To learn more about Jim Brown, visit ABDO Publishing Company online at **www.abdopublishing.com**. Web sites about Jim Brown are featured on our Book Links page. These links are routinely monitored and updated to provide the most current information available.

PLACES TO VISIT

Cleveland Browns Training Camp
77 Lou Groza Boulevard, Berea, OH 44017
440-891-5000
www.clevelandbrowns.com/schedule-and-events/training-camp
Fans of the Cleveland Browns can watch practices for free during training camp.

FirstEnergy Stadium
100 Alfred Lerner Way, Cleveland, OH 44114
440-891-5001
www.clevelandbrowns.com/stadium/index.html
The FirstEnergy Stadium is where the Browns play their exhibition and regular-season home games.

Pro Football Hall of Fame
2121 George Halas Drive Northwest, Canton, OH 44708
330-456-8207
www.profootballhof.com/default.aspx
The Pro Football Hall of Fame features the greatest players and moments in the history of the NFL. Visitors will find exhibits and information on Hall of Fame players, including Brown, who was inducted in 1971.

SOURCE NOTES

CHAPTER 1. Rushing to a Championship

1. Mike Freeman. *Jim Brown: The Fierce Life of an American Hero*. New York: William Morrow, 2006. Print. 161.

2. Ibid. 162.

3. Charles Heaton. "Browns Win, 52–20, for Title." *Cleveland Plain Dealer*. Northeast Ohio Media Group, 13 Dec. 1964. Web. 12 May 2013.

CHAPTER 2. Strong from the Start

1. Mike Freeman. *Jim Brown: The Fierce Life of an American Hero*. New York: William Morrow, 2006. Print. 60.

2. Natalie A. Valentine. "Jim Brown." *Syracuse University Magazine*. Syracuse University Magazine, 1996. Web. 21 May 2013.

3. "A Day and Night with Jim Brown at Williams." *Williams Athletics*. Williams College, 30 Oct. 2009. Web. 16 May 2013.

4. Ibid.

CHAPTER 3. Dominating the Competition

1. George Vecsey. "Jim Brown, Still a Hometown Hero." *New York Times*. New York Times Company, 30 Apr. 2013. Web. 21 May 2013.

2. Mike Freeman. *Jim Brown: The Fierce Life of an American Hero*. New York: William Morrow, 2006. Print. 76.

3. Ibid. 78.

4. Ibid. 81.

5. Ibid. 82.

CHAPTER 4. Life as an Orangeman

1. Natalie A. Valentine. "Jim Brown." *Syracuse University Magazine*. Syracuse University Magazine, 1996. Web. 21 May 2013.

2. Mike Freeman. *Jim Brown: The Fierce Life of an American Hero*. New York: William Morrow, 2006. Print. 85.

3. Ibid. 91.

4. Bud Poliquin. "Poliquin: A Reader Has Asked about Jim Brown, and We Have Tried to Answer." *Syracuse Post-Standard*. Syracuse Media Group, 4 Mar. 2013. Web. 23 May 2013.

5. Ibid.

6. Mike Freeman. *Jim Brown: The Fierce Life of an American Hero*. New York: William Morrow, 2006. Print. 93.

CHAPTER 5. Playing in the NFL

1. Chuck Heaton. "Penn State's Plum Is Ace Passer and Kicker." *Cleveland Plain Dealer*. Northeast Ohio Media Group, 28 Nov. 1956. Web. 23 May 2013.

2. Jim Brown with Steve Delsohn. *Out of Bounds*. New York: Kensington, 1989. Print. 56.

3. Mike Freeman. *Jim Brown: The Fierce Life of an American Hero*. New York: William Morrow, 2006. Print. 105.

4. Jim Brown with Steve Delsohn. *Out of Bounds*. New York: Kensington, 1989. Print. 60.

5. Ibid. 62.

6. Tex Maule. "The Browns' Jim Dandy." *SI Vault*. Time Inc., 10 Nov. 1958. Web. 24 May 2013.

7. Mike Freeman. *Jim Brown: The Fierce Life of an American Hero*. New York: William Morrow, 2006. Print. 108.

8. Bob Hertzel. "Hertzel Column: Orange Up There with Biggest Rivals." *Times West Virginian*. Community Newspaper Holdings, 29 Dec. 2012. Web. 25 May 2013.

9. Ibid.

CHAPTER 6. Leading the Game

1. Mike Freeman. *Jim Brown: The Fierce Life of an American Hero.* New York: William Morrow, 2006. Print. 120.

2. Keith Yowell. "1961: Jim Brown Ties Rushing Record as Browns Crush Eagles." *Today in Pro Football History.* n.p., 19 Nov. 2011. Web. 25 May 2013.

3. Bob Carter. "Davis Won Heisman, Respect." *ESPN Classic.* ESPN.com, n.d. Web. 26 May 2013.

4. Jim Brown with Steve Delsohn. *Out of Bounds.* New York: Kensington, 1989. Print. 105.

5. David C. Ogden and Joel Nathan Rosen. *Fame to Infamy: Race, Sport, and the Fall from Grace.* Jackson: University of Mississippi, 2010.

CHAPTER 7. Forging a New Life

1. Ralph Wiley. "Nobody Else Is Jim Brown." *ESPN Page 2.* ESPN.com, n.d. Web. 9 June 2013.

2. Mike Freeman. *Jim Brown: The Fierce Life of an American Hero.* New York: William Morrow, 2006. Print. 15–16.

3. Alex Haley. "Alex Haley Interviews Jim Brown." *Alex Haley Tribute Site.* Darren Desepoli, Feb. 1968. Web. 26 May 2013.

4. Ibid.

5. Mike Freeman. *Jim Brown: The Fierce Life of an American Hero.* New York: William Morrow, 2006. Print. 200–201.

CHAPTER 8. From Movies to Amer-I-Can

1. Mike Freeman. *Jim Brown: The Fierce Life of an American Hero*. New York: William Morrow, 2006. Print. 217.

2. Yussuf J. Simmonds. "Jim Brown." *Los Angeles Sentinel*. Los Angeles Sentinel. 17 Feb. 2011. Web. 9 June 2013.

3. Megan Rosenfeld. "Jim Brown's Tale of Sex, Football, Sex, Life and Sex." *Los Angeles Times*. Los Angeles Times, 15 Sept. 1989. Web. 9 June 2013.

4. Mike Freeman. *Jim Brown: The Fierce Life of an American Hero*. New York: William Morrow, 2006. Print. 270.

5. Ibid. 265–266.

CHAPTER 9. Back with the Browns

1. Mike Freeman. *Jim Brown: The Fierce Life of an American Hero*. New York: William Morrow, 2006. Print. 236.

2. Ibid.

3. Natalie A. Valentine. "Jim Brown." *Syracuse University Magazine*. Syracuse University Magazine, 1996. Web. 21 May 2013.

4. Mike Freeman. *Jim Brown: The Fierce Life of an American Hero*. New York: William Morrow, 2006. Print. 262.

5. Mike Freeman. "Jim Brown Is a Prisoner on His Own Terms." *New York Times*. New York Times Company, 28 Mar. 2002. Web. 26 May 2013.

6. Jeff Schudel. "Jim Brown Hoping to Mend Differences with Browns President Mike Holmgren." *News-Herald*. News-Herald. 21 Sept. 2012. Web. 14 June 2013.

7. Jamison Hensley. "Jim Brown Reunites with Browns." *ESPN NFL*. ESPN.com. 29 May 2013. Web. 13 June 2013.

INDEX

ABOUT THE AUTHOR

Marty Gitlin is a freelance writer based in Cleveland, Ohio. He has written more than 70 nonfiction educational books for middle school, high school, and college students. Gitlin has won more than 45 awards during his 30 years as a writer, including first place for General Excellence from the Associated Press. That organization also named him as one of the top four feature writers in Ohio.

PHOTO CREDITS